Intelligent Sex

10 Sexual Pleasure For

Long Lasting Relationship.

Lynda Dixon

CONTENTS

Intelligent Sex   **1**
10 Sexual Pleasure For   **1**
Long Lasting Relationship.   **1**
CONTENTS   **3**
INTRODUCTION   **5**
CHAPTER 1   **13**
Communication and Emotional Connection. 13
   :Nurturing Emotional Intimacy.   13
   :Communicating Desires and Needs.   16
CHAPTER 2   **23**
Trust and Vulnerability   23
   :Building Trust in Intimate Settings.   23
   :Embracing Vulnerability for Deeper
Connection.   27
CHAPTER 3   **33**
Sensual Exploration and   33
Foreplay   33
   :Exploring Sensual Pleasures Together.   33
   :The Art of Foreplay: Igniting Passion.   37
CHAPTER 4   43
Variety and   Spontaneity   42
   :Embracing Variety in Intimate Encounters.
43
CHAPTER 5:   **50**
Mutual Satisfaction and Pleasure   50
   :Prioritizing Mutual Satisfaction.   50

CHAPTER 6   **60**

Role of Physical Touch Sensuality.   60

:Power of Physical Touch in. Relationships.   60

:Cultivating Sensuality Beyond Sex.   64

INTELLIGENT   **71**

SEX   **71**

CHAPTER 7   **72**

Exploration and Openness   72

:Encouraging Exploration and Openness. 72

:Embracing New Experiences Together.   76

CHAPTER 8:   **81**

Intimate Connection Beyond the Bedroom.   81

:Strengthening Intimate Bonds Beyond Sex. 81

:Integrating Emotional Connection in daily Life.   85

CHAPTER 9:   **91**

Patience and Adaptability   91

:Adaptability Navigating Changes Together. 95

CHAPTER 10   **101**

Continued Growth and Learning.   101

:Commitment to Continued Growth as a Couple.   101

In conclusion   **114**

INTRODUCTION

In the intricate dance of relationships, intimacy and sexual connection play pivotal roles in fostering enduring bonds. Welcome to the exploration of "Intelligent sex: 10 Sexual Pleasures for Long-Lasting Relationships," a guide illuminating the path toward a deeper, more fulfilling connection between partners. Within the tapestry of human relationships, sexual intimacy is a dynamic thread, interwoven with emotional resonance, trust, and understanding.

This guide transcends the conventional narrative of sex, delving into the realms of intimacy that nurture the longevity of relationships. It's a nuanced exploration of sensual pleasures, steering away from mere physical gratification to embrace the holistic essence of sexual union.

"Intelligent Sex" isn't just about immediate gratification but seeks to unravel the intricacies of sustaining passion and pleasure over time. It's an ode to the diverse facets of intimacy, offering a roadmap for couples seeking to enrich their bond, reignite desire, and navigate the ebbs and flows of their sexual journey.

Throughout this exploration, we'll navigate ten pillars of sexual pleasure, each designed to deepen the connection, ignite passion, and fortify the emotional foundation of relationships. Join in this voyage as we uncover the secrets to fostering a satisfying, enduring, and profoundly fulfilling sexual intimacy that transcends the bounds of time.

INTELLIGENT

SEX

What is Intelligent sex?

Intelligent sex goes beyond

the conventional notions of physical

intimacy, presenting a holistic and

enriching approach to the art of

connection within romantic relationships.

It encapsulates a profound

understanding of both partners' desires,

emphasizing emotional and mental

harmony alongside physical pleasure.

This concept values open

communication, empathy, and mutual

respect as cornerstones, fostering an

environment where both individuals

actively contribute to the dynamics of

their shared sexual experiences.

In the realm of intelligent sex, pleasure

becomes a nuanced exploration,

acknowledging the diversity of desires

and preferences that contribute to a

fulfilling connection. It thrives on

continuous communication,encouraging

couples to engage in an ongoing

dialogue about their evolving needs and

fantasies. This approach appreciates

the importance of consent, ensuring that

boundaries are respected, and both

partners feel secure in expressing their

vulnerabilities and desires.

Intelligent sex is a dynamic journey that evolves with the relationship, integrating creativity, trust, and adaptability. It transforms the physical act into an emotionally resonant experience, where each encounter deepens the bond between partners. This introduction aims to shed light on the multifaceted nature of intelligent sex, positioning it as a conscious and evolving exploration that contributes to the enduring vitality of long-lasting relationships.

INTELLIGENT

SEX

CHAPTER 1

Communication and Emotional Connection.

:Nurturing Emotional Intimacy.

Nurturing emotional intimacy forms the bedrock of enduring and profound connections within relationships. It transcends mere verbal exchanges, encompassing a realm where partners cultivate a deep understanding of each other's inner worlds, vulnerabilities, and emotions.

At its core, nurturing emotional intimacy involves fostering an environment of trust, empathy, and unwavering support. It's about creating a safe space where individuals feel empowered to express their truest selves without fear of judgment. Communication becomes a channel for sharing aspirations, fears, joys, and disappointments, fostering a sense of mutual understanding and respect.

This intimacy thrives on active listening and genuine empathy, allowing partners to attune themselves to each other's emotional needs and respond with compassion. It's about being present—both physically and emotionally—through moments of joy and adversity, offering unwavering support and validation.

Cultivating emotional intimacy necessitates the willingness to be vulnerable, to share fears and dreams openly. It involves creating rituals of connection, whether through shared experiences, deep conversations, or simple gestures that reaffirm the bond.

Ultimately, nurturing emotional intimacy within a relationship is a continuous, intentional effort. It builds bridges between hearts, strengthening the foundation upon which lasting love and profound connections flourish, enhancing the depth and resilience of the partnership.

:Communicating Desires and Needs.

In relationships, the art of communicating desires and needs forms a cornerstone for mutual understanding and fulfillment. It involves the ability to articulate one's emotional, physical, and intimate requirements openly and respectfully.

Authentic communication of desires and needs begins with self-awareness. Understanding personal desires and needs lays the groundwork for effectively expressing them to a partner. This involves introspection, recognizing individual preferences, boundaries, and aspirations within the relationship.

Expressing these desires and needs requires clarity and honesty. It involves creating a space where both partners feel comfortable sharing without fear of judgment or rejection. Effective communication involves active listening, allowing both individuals to comprehend and acknowledge each other's perspectives without defensiveness. Articulating desires and needs isn't solely about stating them but also understanding the context and emotions behind them. It's crucial to convey not just the "what" but the "why" and "how" of these desires, fostering a deeper comprehension of their significance. Moreover, openness to compromise and negotiation plays a pivotal role. It involves finding a middle ground where both partners' needs are considered, fostering a sense of mutual satisfaction and understanding.

When desires and needs are communicated effectively, it fosters a climate of trust and empathy within the relationship. It nurtures an environment where both individuals feel valued, respected, and heard, ultimately leading to greater intimacy, connection, and fulfillment between partners.

"In the realm of intelligent sex,

communication is the bridge between

desire and fulfillment, a fluent exchange

of needs and vulnerabilities that

deepens connection. It's a shared

language, where partners articulate their

desires, building a profound

understanding that transforms each

encounter into an intimate dialogue.

Intelligent sex thrives on this connection,

where open communication becomes

the heartbeat of a shared journey

towards mutual satisfaction and

emotional resonance."

CHAPTER 2

Trust and Vulnerability

:Building Trust in Intimate Settings.

Building trust in intimate settings lays the foundation for a deeply connected and resilient relationship. It involves establishing a safe and secure environment where vulnerability is welcomed and respected.

At the core of building trust lies honesty and transparency. It's about being authentic in words and actions, aligning behavior with intentions. Consistency in behavior cultivates reliability, nurturing a sense of dependability crucial for fostering trust in intimate settings.

Effective communication plays a pivotal role. It involves actively listening to each other's concerns, fears, and vulnerabilities without judgment. Creating a space where partners feel heard and understood enhances trust, encouraging the sharing of intimate thoughts and feelings.

Respecting boundaries is equally vital. Recognizing and honoring each other's limits and comfort zones fosters a sense of safety within intimate interactions. It's about demonstrating respect for personal space and emotional autonomy.

Demonstrating reliability and dependability amplifies trust. Keeping promises, being present in times of need, and offering unwavering support reaffirm the reliability of the relationship, nurturing a sense of security and trust.

Forging trust in intimate settings also involves acknowledging mistakes and addressing conflicts constructively. It's about taking accountability, resolving issues respectfully, and learning and growing together from these experiences.

Ultimately, building trust in intimate settings is an ongoing process that requires patience, empathy, and a commitment to nurturing the emotional safety of the relationship. When trust flourishes, it becomes the bedrock upon which deep intimacy and enduring connections thrive.

:Embracing Vulnerability for Deeper Connection.

Embracing vulnerability within a relationship is the gateway to fostering a deeper, more profound connection between partners. It involves the courage to reveal one's authentic self, complete with fears, insecurities, and emotions, creating an atmosphere of openness and trust.

Vulnerability isn't a sign of weakness but rather a display of courage and authenticity. It requires a willingness to shed masks and share genuine emotions, thoughts, and fears with a partner. By allowing oneself to be vulnerable, individuals invite their partners into their inner worlds, creating a space for empathy, understanding, and emotional resonance.

This act of vulnerability nurtures an environment where both partners feel safe to express themselves fully. It opens the door to deeper emotional connections, fostering empathy and a profound sense of intimacy. Sharing vulnerabilities creates a bond built on trust and mutual support, strengthening the emotional foundation of the relationship.

Embracing vulnerability also entails actively listening and empathizing with a partner's vulnerabilities. It involves offering compassion and support, creating a reciprocal exchange of openness and understanding within the relationship.

Moreover, vulnerability fosters growth and resilience. It allows partners to navigate challenges together, learn from shared experiences, and evolve as individuals and as a couple.

In essence, embracing vulnerability is an essential element in creating a deeper connection. It's the raw and unfiltered expression of oneself that paves the way for profound emotional intimacy and a stronger, more enduring bond between partners.

"*In intelligent sex, trust is the unspoken pact, creating a sanctuary where vulnerability becomes the canvas for profound connection. It's a dance ofintimacy where trust and vulnerability intertwine, weaving a tapestry of shared desires Through and unguarded*"

passion. this delicate interplay, intelligent sex emerges as an art form that blossoms in the tender embrace of mutual trust and open vulnerability."

CHAPTER 3

Sensual Exploration and

Foreplay

:Exploring Sensual Pleasures Together.

Exploring sensual pleasures together within a relationship is an enchanting journey that transcends physicality, delving into the realms of shared intimacy and connection. It involves a mutual exploration of the senses, fostering a deeper understanding of each other's desires and preferences.

This exploration begins with open communication and a willingness to embark on a joint journey of discovery. Partners engage in conversations about sensual preferences, fantasies, and interests, creating a roadmap for shared experiences that heighten intimacy.

It involves indulging in sensory experiences that ignite passion and pleasure, whether through touch, taste, sight, scent, or sound. From experimenting with different textures and sensations to savoring exotic flavors together, each exploration deepens the bond between partners.

Shared sensual experiences encompass more than physical touch. They extend to creating a conducive atmosphere, setting the stage for intimate encounters—be it through ambiance, lighting, or incorporating elements that evoke heightened sensations and emotions.

This journey of exploration is a space free from judgment, encouraging partners to venture beyond their comfort zones while respecting each other's boundaries. It's an opportunity to experiment, learn, and grow together, fostering a sense of adventure and novelty within the relationship.

Furthermore, exploring sensual pleasures together nurtures a deeper connection by fostering empathy and understanding. It enhances the emotional resonance between partners, strengthening the intimacy and passion that form the fabric of a fulfilling and enduring relationship.

:The Art of Foreplay: Igniting Passion.

The art of foreplay embodies the intricate dance of anticipation, teasing, and emotional connection, serving as a catalyst to ignite a blaze of passion and intimacy within a relationship. It's more than a prelude to sex; it's an immersive experience that sets the stage for a profound and fulfilling connection between partners.

Foreplay isn't solely about physical stimulation but encompasses a holistic approach to intimacy. It involves engaging all the senses—touch, taste, sight, scent, and sound—to create a rich tapestry of sensations that heighten arousal and deepen the emotional bond. Communication becomes pivotal in the art of foreplay. Partners openly share desires, fantasies, and preferences, creating a roadmap for exploration that caters to each other's needs and pleasures. This exchange of desires fosters a deeper understanding, guiding the way to satisfying and passionate encounters.

Variety and creativity play a crucial role. Foreplay isn't confined to a singular routine but encourages experimentation with different techniques, gestures, and activities that build anticipation and excitement. It's about exploring erogenous zones, engaging in sensual massages, engaging in verbal or non-verbal cues, and relishing the thrill of anticipation.

Furthermore, the art of foreplay thrives on mindfulness and presence. It involves being attuned to each other's responses, adapting and responding to cues, and relishing the shared experience of building desire and connection.

Ultimately, the art of foreplay isn't just a prelude; it's an integral part of fostering deep emotional and physical intimacy. When executed with care, creativity, and genuine desire to connect, it serves as a powerful means to ignite and sustain passion within a relationship.

"Sensual exploration in intelligent sex is the delicate dance of discovery, where every touch unveils a new dimension of desire. Foreplay becomes the poetic prelude, setting the stage for a symphony of sensations that resonate through the artful exchange of pleasure.In this realm, each caress and

whispered anticipation becomes an essential note in the composition of intimate connection."

CHAPTER 4

Variety and Spontaneity

:Embracing Variety in Intimate Encounters.

Embracing variety in intimate encounters within a relationship enriches the tapestry of shared experiences, fostering excitement, novelty, and deeper connections between partners. It involves an openness to explore diverse expressions of intimacy, keeping the flame of passion alive and thriving.

Variety brings a sense of adventure and spontaneity to intimate moments. It encompasses an array of experiences, from trying new positions and techniques to incorporating playful elements that infuse an air of excitement and anticipation into the relationship.

This embracement of variety extends beyond physical acts to encompass emotional and psychological facets. It encourages partners to delve into different ways of expressing desire, love, and affection, nurturing a multifaceted connection that evolves and grows over time.

Moreover, variety in intimate encounters requires open communication and a willingness to explore each other's fantasies and desires. It's about creating a safe space where partners feel comfortable expressing their preferences without judgment, allowing for mutual understanding and the discovery of new pleasures together.

Variety in intimacy also rejuvenates the relationship by breaking routine and monotony. It injects freshness into the partnership, reigniting passion and keeping both partners engaged and excited about each other.

Embracing variety in intimate encounters is a testament to the adaptability and dynamism of the relationship. It celebrates the uniqueness of each moment and contributes to the vibrancy and longevity of the bond between partners, fostering a deeper, more fulfilling connection in their shared journey of intimacy.

:Spontaneity: Keeping Desire Alive.

Spontaneity serves as a catalyst in relationships, injecting an element of surprise, excitement, and passion that keeps desire alive and thriving. It's the art of embracing the unexpected, infusing moments with a sense of adventure and novelty, reigniting the spark between partners. In relationships, routines can sometimes dim the flame of desire. Spontaneity, however, breaks free from predictability, introducing an element of surprise that catches partners off guard in the most delightful ways. Whether it's a spontaneous romantic gesture, an unplanned getaway, or an unexpected intimate moment, spontaneity keeps the relationship dynamic and invigorating. This element of surprise fuels anticipation and excitement. It keeps partners engaged and intrigued by each other, fostering a sense of curiosity and interest that sustains desire. Spontaneous acts express a partner's Ultimately, spontaneity is the secret ingredient that keeps desire alive inrelationships. Its ability to infuse moments with excitement and novelty helps sustain the passion, ensuring that

the flames of desire continue to burn

brightly between partners.

"Intelligent sex thrives on the canvas of variety, where each encounter paints a unique masterpiece of desire. Spontaneity is the brushstroke that brings passion to life, ensuring that intimacy is a dynamic and ever-evolving journey within the realm of profound connection."

CHAPTER 5:

Mutual Satisfaction and Pleasure

:Prioritizing Mutual Satisfaction.

Prioritizing mutual satisfaction within a relationship lays the groundwork for a fulfilling and harmonious connection between partners. It involves a shared commitment to understanding and fulfilling each other's desires, needs, and pleasures, fostering a deep sense of emotional and physical fulfillment.

At the heart of prioritizing mutual satisfaction lies open communication. Partners engage in candid discussions about their preferences, fantasies, and boundaries, creating a platform for understanding and catering to each other's desires. This dialogue fosters a deeper connection, allowing both individuals to actively participate in ensuring each other's satisfaction.

This prioritization isn't just about physical pleasure; it encompasses emotional fulfillment as well. It involves attending to each other's emotional needs, offering support, reassurance, and nurturing a sense of security within the relationship.

Respect for each other's pleasure becomes paramount. Partners prioritize mutual satisfaction by valuing and respecting each other's boundaries and comfort levels, ensuring that all intimate encounters are consensual and enjoyable for both parties involved.

Moreover, it involves a genuine investment in exploring and fulfilling each other's desires. This commitment to mutual satisfaction encourages experimentation, trying new experiences, and being receptive to each other's suggestions, fostering an atmosphere of shared pleasure and fulfillment.

Prioritizing mutual satisfaction ultimately strengthens the bond between partners. It fosters a sense of equality, reciprocity, and consideration, ensuring that both individuals feel valued and cherished within the relationship. When both partners actively work towards each other's satisfaction, it creates a deeply fulfilling and enduring connection built on mutual respect and understanding.

:Enhancing Pleasure for Both Partners.

Enhancing pleasure for both partners within a relationship is a collaborative journey that revolves around ensuring mutual satisfaction and fulfillment. It's about creating an environment where both individuals feel valued and their needs and desires are equally prioritized, fostering a harmonious and deeply gratifying connection.

Effective communication forms the cornerstone of enhancing pleasure. Partners engage in open and honest conversations about their preferences, fantasies, and boundaries. This dialogue allows for a deeper understanding of each other's desires, paving the way for tailored experiences that bring pleasure to both individuals.

Reciprocity plays a crucial role. Each partner takes an active role in ensuring the other's pleasure, understanding that mutual enjoyment enhances the overall experience. It involves attentiveness and responsiveness to each other's cues and signals, creating an atmosphere where both individuals feel seen and attended to.

Exploration and experimentation contribute to enhancing pleasure. Partners actively seek new ways to satisfy each other's desires, whether through trying different techniques, positions, or incorporating novel elements into intimate encounters. This willingness to explore fosters excitement and novelty, amplifying pleasure for both partners.

Furthermore, an emphasis on equality and balance contributes to enhanced pleasure. Partners ensure that both individuals receive equal attention, satisfaction, and pleasure, creating a sense of fairness and fulfillment within the relationship.

Ultimately, enhancing pleasure for both partners creates a mutually satisfying and enriching dynamic. It strengthens the emotional and physical connection between partners, fostering a relationship where the pursuit of pleasure becomes a collaborative and joyful endeavor, nurturing a deeply fulfilling and lasting bond.

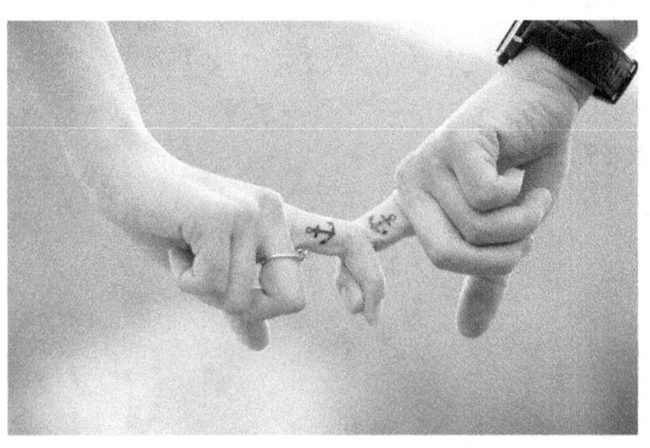

"In the realm of intelligent sex, mutual satisfaction is the shared melody, resonating between partners, orchestrating a harmonious symphony of pleasure. It's a dance of reciprocity

where both find fulfillment, turning moments of intimacy into a shared masterpiece of joy. Intelligent sex, at its core, is the art of crafting satisfaction as a collaborative expression of love and connection."

CHAPTER 6

Role of Physical Touch Sensuality.

:Power of Physical Touch in. Relationships.

The power of physical touch within relationships transcends mere sensation; it serves as a profound means of communication, connection, and emotional bonding between partners. Touch is a universal language that conveys care, love, empathy, and support, nurturing a deeper sense of intimacy and understanding.

Physical touch serves as a powerful tool for expressing emotions when words fall short. It communicates affection, reassurance, and empathy, bridging emotional gaps and fostering a sense of closeness between partners. From a gentle caress to a warm embrace, each touch carries with it the ability to convey love and support in ways that words often struggle to articulate.

Moreover, the impact of physical touch on emotional well-being is profound. It releases oxytocin, the "bonding hormone," reducing stress, enhancing feelings of trust, and promoting emotional stability within the relationship. Simple acts like holding hands, hugs, or cuddling not only bring physical comfort but also strengthen the emotional connection between partners. Physical touch also serves as a medium for pleasure and intimacy. From passionate moments to tender gestures, it plays a pivotal role in igniting desire, strengthening the sexual bond, and fostering a sense of mutual satisfaction and fulfillment within the relationship.

Furthermore, touch contributes to a sense of safety and security. A reassuring touch during moments of distress or a comforting embrace signifies solidarity and support, creating an environment where both partners feel emotionally supported and understood.

In essence, the power of physical touch in relationships is multifaceted. It communicates love, empathy, and support, enhances emotional well-being, fosters intimacy, and creates a profound connection that enriches the fabric of the relationship, nurturing a deeper sense of love and understanding between partners.

:Cultivating Sensuality Beyond Sex.

Cultivating sensuality beyond the realm of sex involves embracing a holistic approach to intimacy, exploring a spectrum of experiences that enrich the emotional and physical connection between partners. It's about fostering an environment where sensuality becomes an integral part of everyday interactions, transcending the confines of the bedroom.

Sensuality in daily life revolves around engaging the senses in various non-sexual ways. It encompasses acts that evoke pleasure, intimacy, and emotional connection, such as sharing meaningful conversations, enjoying leisurely moments together, or indulging in activities that stimulate the senses, like cooking together, dancing, or even engaging in mutual hobbies.

The art of touch plays a pivotal role in cultivating sensuality. Non-sexual physical touch, such as holding hands, giving massages, or gentle caresses, communicates intimacy and fosters a deeper emotional connection outside of sexual encounters.

Creating a conducive atmosphere also contributes to cultivating sensuality. Partners may focus on enhancing the ambiance—through lighting, music, or even scents—that fosters relaxation, comfort, and a sense of intimacy, creating opportunities for sensuous experiences in everyday settings.

Mindfulness and presence are essential. Being fully present in each moment allows partners to appreciate the subtleties of sensory experiences, deepening the connection and intimacy between them.

Moreover, cultivating sensuality beyond sex involves continuous exploration and creativity. Partners experiment with different ways to evoke sensual experiences, finding new avenues to stimulate the senses and infuse their relationship with passion, joy, and emotional richness.

Ultimately, cultivating sensuality beyond sex enriches the relationship by infusing it with moments of connection, pleasure, and intimacy. It creates a tapestry of experiences that nurture a deeper, more fulfilling bond between partners, fostering a relationship where sensuality becomes an integral and cherished aspect of their shared journey.

"In the integration of sex, physical touch becomes the artful expression of sensuality, a tactile language that communicates desires with eloquence. Each caress is a brushstroke on thecanvas of intimacy, creating a masterpiece of shared pleasure. Sensuality intertwines with physical touch, forming the essence of a

harmonious dance where bodies speak the language of connection and passion."

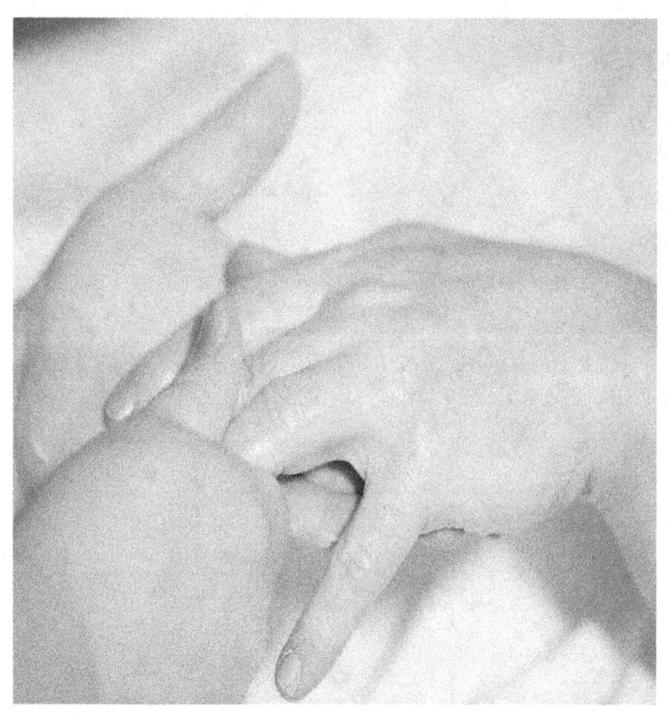

INTELLIGENT

SEX

CHAPTER 7

Exploration and Openness

:Encouraging Exploration and Openness.

Encouraging exploration and openness within a relationship is an invitation to embark on a journey of discovery, growth, and deeper connection. It involves fostering an environment where partners feel empowered and supported to explore new experiences, perspectives, and aspects of themselves.

At its core, encouraging exploration requires a foundation of trust and open communication. Partners create a safe space where they can openly share their thoughts, desires, and curiosities without fear of judgment. This openness lays the groundwork for mutual understanding and the freedom to explore without reservations.

Embracing exploration involves a curiosity to delve into uncharted territories together. Partners encourage each other to try new things, whether it's engaging in novel activities, exploring different aspects of intimacy, or embarking on adventures that foster growth individually and as a couple.

Moreover, fostering openness within the relationship entails a willingness to embrace change and evolution. It involves being adaptable and flexible, allowing room for both partners to grow and evolve while supporting each other's personal development.

Encouraging exploration and openness also requires an appreciation for diversity and differences. Partners celebrate each other's uniqueness, valuing diverse perspectives and experiences that contribute to a rich and dynamic relationship.

Ultimately, fostering exploration and openness creates a space for continuous learning, self-discovery, and mutual growth. It nurtures a relationship where partners feel liberated to express themselves authentically, fostering a deeper sense of connection, understanding, and fulfillment within their shared journey of exploration and discovery.

:Embracing New Experiences Together.

Embracing new experiences together within a relationship is a transformative journey that deepens the bond between partners and enriches the fabric of their connection. It involves a shared commitment to exploring uncharted territories, fostering growth, and creating lasting memories.

At its essence, embracing new experiences is about a joint willingness to step outside the comfort zone. It involves a sense of adventure, openness to trying different activities, and a spirit of curiosity that propels partners into novel and unfamiliar territories.

Shared experiences serve as building blocks for a stronger connection. Whether it's traveling to new destinations, engaging in new hobbies, or simply trying new cuisines, these experiences create shared memories that strengthen the emotional bond and foster a sense of togetherness.

Embracing new experiences together also nurtures personal growth within the relationship. It encourages partners to learn from each other, adapt to new situations, and evolve both individually and as a couple. It's a journey of mutual support and encouragement, facilitating personal development and shared growth.

Moreover, new experiences ignite excitement and passion within the relationship. They infuse a sense of novelty, creating opportunities for shared discovery, laughter, and moments of joy that invigorate the relationship.

Ultimately, embracing new experiences together contributes to the resilience and longevity of the relationship. It cultivates a sense of shared adventure and a spirit of exploration, fostering a deeper emotional connection and creating a treasure trove of shared experiences that become the pillars of a fulfilling and enduring partnership.

"In the realm of intelligent sex, exploration is the compass guiding a journey of mutual discovery, where partners traverse uncharted territories of desire with curiosity and openness. It's an intimate adventure, unraveling layers of pleasure and connection through a shared commitment to *discovery.Openness becomes the key, unlocking the doors to profound intimacy and evolving desires, creating a dynamic landscape of exploration within the context of intelligent*

CHAPTER 8:

Intimate Connection Beyond the Bedroom.

:Strengthening Intimate Bonds Beyond Sex.

Strengthening intimate bonds beyond the realm of sex involves nurturing a profound emotional connection that transcends physical intimacy, enriching the relationship on multiple levels. It encompasses various elements that contribute to a deeper and more enduring closeness between partners.

Communication forms the backbone of strengthening intimate bonds. Partners engage in open and honest conversations, sharing thoughts, fears, dreams, and vulnerabilities. This transparency fosters understanding, empathy, and a sense of closeness, laying the foundation for a deeper emotional connection.

Shared experiences outside of the bedroom play a pivotal role. Engaging in activities that foster emotional intimacy, such as deep conversations, shared hobbies, or simply spending quality time together, solidifies the emotional bond between partners, reinforcing their connection beyond the physical aspect.

Mutual support and empathy further fortify intimate bonds. Being there for each other during challenging times, offering unwavering support, and showing genuine care and understanding enhance the emotional connection, creating a sense of security and trust within the relationship.

Acts of affection and gestures of love outside of sexual encounters contribute significantly. From small acts of kindness to expressing appreciation and affection through words and actions, these moments affirm the emotional connection between partners, strengthening their bond.

Moreover, shared values, mutual respect, and a commitment to each other's well-being deepen the intimate connection.

When partners align in their values and show respect for each other's individuality, it cultivates a sense of unity and mutual understanding that reinforces the intimacy in the relationship.

Ultimately, strengthening intimate bonds beyond sex involves investing time, effort, and care into nurturing the emotional connection. It's about fostering a deep sense of trust, understanding, and love that forms the cornerstone of a fulfilling and lasting partnership.

:Integrating Emotional Connection in daily Life.

Integrating emotional connection into daily life is about weaving threads of understanding, empathy, and affection into the fabric of everyday interactions, creating a nurturing environment that fosters a deep and lasting bond between partners.

Communication becomes a cornerstone in integrating emotional connection. Partners engage in meaningful conversations beyond daily routines, sharing thoughts, feelings, and experiences. This openness builds a bridge of understanding, strengthening the emotional connection and ensuring that both individuals feel heard and valued in their relationship.

Shared rituals and routines play a significant role. From morning routines to bedtime rituals, partners create moments that symbolize their emotional connection—be it sharing meals, walks, or engaging in activities that promote a sense of togetherness, fostering a deeper emotional intimacy.

Expressing affection and appreciation in daily interactions reinforces the emotional connection. Simple gestures like hugs, kisses, or words of encouragement serve as reminders of love and support, nurturing the emotional bond between partners.

Empathy and support during challenging times further integrate emotional connection. Being there for each other, offering comfort, and showing genuine concern and understanding solidify the emotional ties, creating a sense of security and trust in the relationship.

Moreover, integrating emotional connection involves mindfulness and presence. Partners consciously make an effort to be present in moments shared together, valuing the emotional significance of these interactions, and reinforcing their connection through attentive and caring behavior.

Ultimately, integrating emotional connection into daily life transforms mundane moments into opportunities for closeness and understanding. It creates a foundation of emotional security and support, enriching the relationship with depth, resilience, and enduring love.

"Intelligent sex extends its embrace beyond the bedroom, intertwining with daily life as a continuous expression of emotional closeness. It manifests in shared laughter, gentle touches, and the unspoken understanding that permeates mundane moments. In this expansive intimacy, love becomes a constant

thread, weaving through the fabric of routine, fostering a deep and enduring connection that transcends physical encounters."

CHAPTER 9

Patience and Adaptability

:Practicing Patience in Sexual Exploration.

Practicing patience in sexual exploration within a relationship is a testament to understanding, respect, and a commitment to mutual growth and satisfaction. It involves a deliberate and compassionate approach towards discovering each other's desires and boundaries, nurturing a deeper and more fulfilling intimate connection.

Patience in sexual exploration begins with open and honest communication. Partners engage in dialogues that foster understanding, allowing each other the space to express desires, fears, and limitations without pressure or judgment. This patient exchange of thoughts lays the groundwork for a more harmonious and fulfilling exploration.

It involves respecting the pace of each partner's sexual journey. Patience allows for the gradual unfolding of intimacy, acknowledging that everyone's comfort level varies. Partners navigate the exploration process slowly and attentively, ensuring that both individuals feel secure and comfortable every step of the way.

Moreover, patience in sexual exploration entails an openness to learning and adapting. It involves embracing the idea that sexual preferences and desires may evolve over time, and being patient allows for the growth and evolution of these experiences.

Patience also involves embracing moments of vulnerability and setbacks without rushing or pressuring each other. Partners understand that trust and intimacy take time to build and that setbacks are part of the journey. Patience allows for the space to process and navigate these moments together with empathy and support.

Ultimately, practicing patience in sexual exploration cultivates a foundation of trust, respect, and understanding within the relationship. It creates an environment where partners feel safe to explore and express themselves authentically, fostering a deeply satisfying and emotionally connected intimate bond.

:Adaptability   Navigating Changes Together.

Adaptability in a relationship is the cornerstone of navigating life's changes and challenges together. It's the capacity to adjust, evolve, and grow in sync with each other amidst the dynamic nature of life, fostering resilience and unity between partners.

Life is a series of transformations, and adaptability allows couples to weather these changes as a team. It involves a shared mindset that embraces flexibility and openness, acknowledging that growth often involves navigating unfamiliar territories.

Communication plays a pivotal role in adaptability. Partners engage in open discussions, sharing concerns, aspirations, and strategies to cope with change. This dialogue fosters mutual understanding, allowing both individuals to support each other through transitions, be it career shifts, moving homes, or personal growth.

Adaptability requires mutual support and encouragement. Partners stand by each other, offering reassurance, and being flexible in accommodating each other's needs during periods of change. This support creates a sense of security and trust, ensuring that both individuals feel understood and valued in the face of uncertainty.

Moreover, adaptability involves a willingness to learn and grow together. Couples embrace change as an opportunity for personal and relational evolution, adapting their dynamics and perspectives to align with new circumstances.

Patience and empathy are integral aspects of adaptability. Partners recognize that adaptation takes time and effort, respecting each other's pace and providing support through the adjustment process.

Ultimately, adaptability strengthens the bond between partners. It fosters a relationship where both individuals feel empowered to face change as a team, promoting unity, understanding, and resilience in navigating life's transitions together.

"In the realm of intelligent sex, patience is the gentle hand that guides the symphony of connection, allowing desires to unfold organically. Adaptability is the art of harmonizing with the ever-changing rhythms of

passion, ensuring that intimacy evolves gracefully. Together, patience and adaptability create a nuanced dance, where the ebb and flow of pleasure become a testament to the enduring artistry of a truly intelligent and fulfilling sexual experience."

CHAPTER 10

Continued Growth and Learning.

:Commitment to Continued Growth as a Couple.

A commitment to continued growth as a couple signifies an ongoing dedication to evolving together, nurturing the relationship, and deepening the connection over time. It involves a shared understanding that growth isn't limited to individuals but extends to the relationship as an entity that requires care, attention, and nurturing.

This commitment hinges on a mindset of continuous improvement and learning. Couples actively seek opportunities to grow together, whether through shared experiences, seeking new knowledge, or working on aspects of the relationship that could benefit from enhancement.

Communication forms the bedrock of growth as a couple. Partners engage in open dialogues about their aspirations, goals, and areas where they envision the relationship evolving. This ongoing conversation fosters a deeper understanding of each other's needs and desires, setting the stage for mutual growth.

Embracing change becomes a shared value. Couples acknowledge that growth often involves stepping out of comfort zones, adapting to new dynamics, and being receptive to evolving together. They navigate changes as a team, supporting each other through challenges and celebrating milestones together.

Additionally, a commitment to growth involves a willingness to address conflicts constructively. Couples approach disagreements as opportunities for learning and understanding, seeking resolutions that contribute to the relationship's growth and maturity.

This commitment also necessitates making time for the relationship amidst life's demands. Couples prioritize moments together, fostering intimacy, and ensuring that the relationship remains a focal point amid busy schedules.

Ultimately, a commitment to continued growth as a couple fosters a relationship that flourishes over time. It creates an environment where both individuals feel supported, understood, and valued, laying the groundwork for a fulfilling and enduring partnership built on mutual evolution and shared aspirations.

:Embracing Learning and Evolution.

Embracing learning and evolution within a relationship signifies a commitment to growth, adaptability, and the continuous exploration of new facets within the partnership. It's an acknowledgment that both individuals and the relationship itself are in a constant state of flux, and embracing this process fosters a deeper, more resilient connection.

Learning and evolution involve an openness to new experiences. Partners actively seek opportunities to expand their horizons together, whether through shared activities, travel, or discovering new hobbies. This curiosity fuels personal growth and strengthens the bond between partners.

Communication becomes a gateway to learning and evolution. Couples engage in meaningful discussions about their aspirations, desires, and areas for improvement within the relationship. This dialogue creates an environment of understanding and mutual support, enabling both individuals to evolve together.

Adaptability is a key component. Embracing evolution means being flexible and open-minded in navigating changes, be they external circumstances or shifts in personal perspectives. Couples support each other through these transitions, fostering a sense of unity and resilience.

Self-reflection and introspection play a significant role. Partners actively reflect on their individual growth, encouraging personal development while also being attuned to the evolution of the relationship as a whole.

Embracing learning and evolution involves a willingness to learn from challenges. Couples approach difficulties as opportunities for growth, utilizing them as lessons to strengthen the relationship's foundation and deepen their connection.

Ultimately, embracing learning and evolution cultivates a relationship that thrives on growth and mutual support. It creates an environment where both individuals feel empowered to learn, adapt, and evolve together, fostering a relationship that continues to blossom and flourish over time.

"Intelligent sex is a journey of continued growth and learning, where partners evolve together, exploring new dimensions of desire and intimacy. It's a shared commitment to understanding each other's evolving needs, creating a dynamic space for ongoing exploration.

In this realm, the pursuit of knowledge becomes an integral part of the intimate connection, fostering a deepening bond that thrives on the curiosity to discover and fulfill each other's desires."

INTELLIGENT

SEX

NOTES

In conclusion

Intelligent sex encompasses various aspects, fostering not just sexual pleasure but also nurturing long-lasting relationships. It integrates communication, consent, and understanding, elevating physical intimacy into a profound emotional connection. Prioritizing pleasure isn't just about physical satisfaction but about mutual respect, exploring desires, and fostering trust. It's about building an enduring connection, where both partners feel valued, understood, and fulfilled. In essence, the pursuit of sexual pleasure within a relationship is a journey that requires empathy, open communication, and continuous efforts to deepen emotional bonds while enjoying physical intimacy.